EARTH'S BIGGEST SHOW-OFFS

The most SPECTACULAR NATURAL WONDERS on the planet

By Andy Seed

Illustrated by Sam Caldwell

happy yak

For everyone at Coalway Junior School – A.S.

For Isla – S.C.

© 2025 Quarto Publishing plc.
Text © 2025 Andy Seed
Illustrations © 2025 Sam Caldwell

First published in 2025 by Happy Yak, an imprint of The Quarto Group.
1 Triptych Place, London, SE1 9SH, UK.
T (0)20 7700 6700 F (0)20 7700 8066
EEA Representation, WTS Tax d.o.o., Žanova ulica 3, 4000 Kranj, Slovenia.
www.quarto.com

Andy Seed has asserted his right to be identified as the author of this work.
Sam Caldwell has asserted his right to be identified as the illustrator of this work.

All rights reserved.

No part of this publication may be reproduced, stored in a retrieval system, or transmitted in any form, or by any means, electrical, mechanical, photocopying, recording or otherwise, without the prior written permission of the publisher or a licence permitting restricted copying. In the United Kingdom such licences are issued by the Copyright Licensing Agency, 5th Floor, Shackleton House, 4 Battle Bridge Lane, London SE1 2HX.

A catalogue record for this book is available from the British Library.

ISBN 978-1-83600-009-9
eISBN 978-1-83600-012-9

Designer: Victoria Vassiades
Editor: Amanda Askew
Consultant: Priyanka Lamichhane
Commissioning Editor: Catharine Robertson
Senior Designer: Sarah Chapman-Suire
Creative Director: Malena Stojić
Associate Publisher: Rhiannon Findlay
Senior Production Controller: Elizabeth Reardon

Printed in Malaysia COS032025

9 8 7 6 5 4 3 2 1

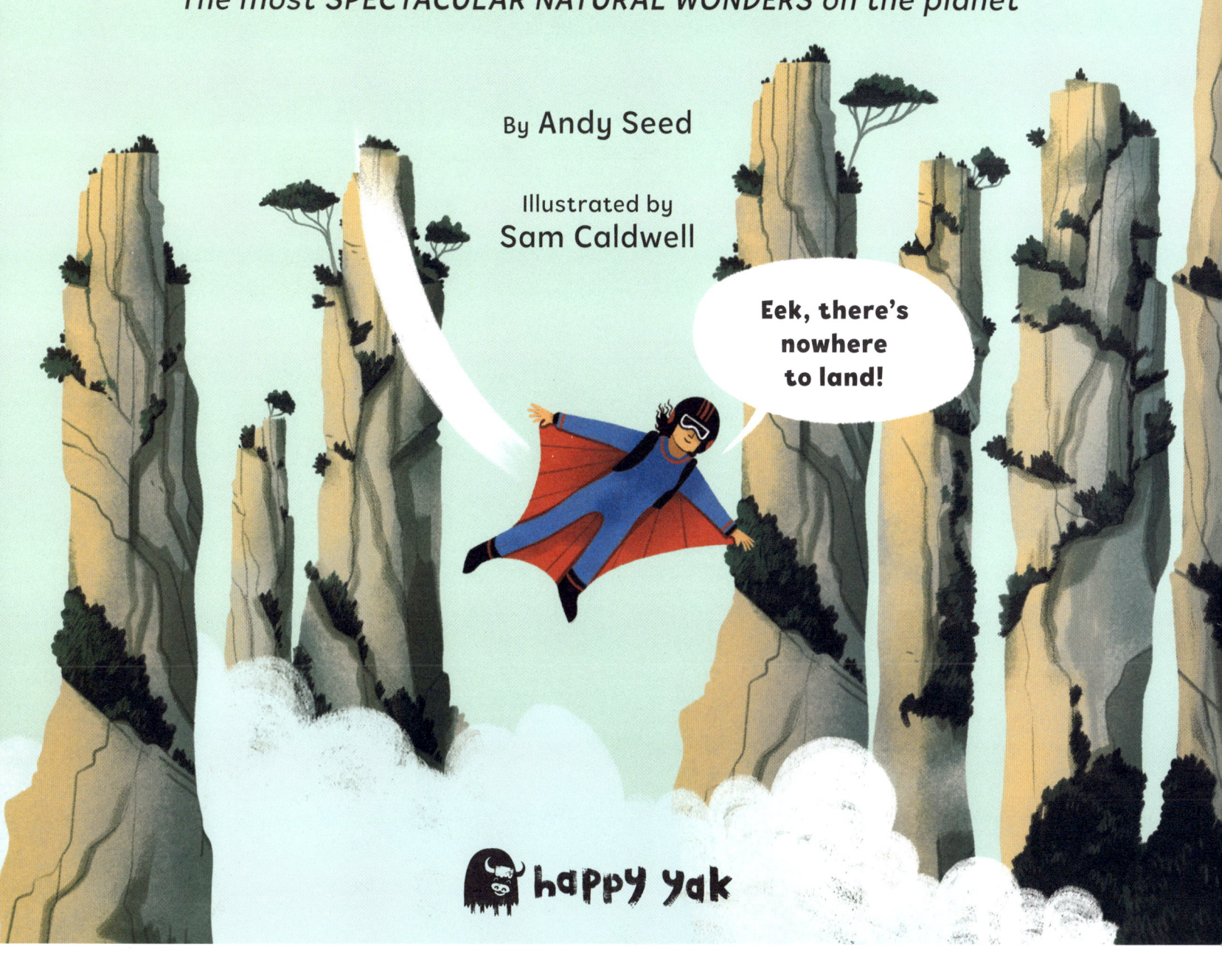

CONTENTS

HIGH AND MIGHTY

10 ✦ Mount Everest
12 ✦ Uluṟu
13 ✦ Perito Moreno Glacier

14 ✦ **TOP FIVE:**
Colossal Cliffs

16 ✦ Mount Kilimanjaro
17 ✦ Mauna Kea

18 ✦ **THE BATTLE OF THE VOLCANOES:**
Parícutin vs Vesuvius

20 ✦ Sossusvlei Sand Dunes
21 ✦ Dolomites

WET AND WILD

24 ✦ Nazaré Surf
25 ✦ Lake Baikal
26 ✦ Great Barrier Reef

28 ✦ **THE BATTLE OF THE MIGHTY RIVERS:**
Amazon vs Nile

30 ✦ Iguazu Falls
31 ✦ Dead Sea
32 ✦ Pamukkale
33 ✦ Lake Hillier

DEEP AND DANGEROUS

36 ✦ Grand Canyon
38 ✦ Padirac Caves
39 ✦ Meteor Crater

---

40 ✦ **TOP FIVE:**
Astonishing Islands

---

42 ✦ Zhangjiajie Pillars
43 ✦ Mariana Trench

---

44 ✦ **THE BATTLE OF THE GEYSERS:**
Geysir vs Pohutu

VAST AND VARIED

48 ✦ Amazon Rainforest
50 ✦ Aurora Borealis
51 ✦ Salar de Uyuni
52 ✦ Iceberg A23a
54 ✦ Sahara Desert
56 ✦ Giant's Causeway
57 ✦ Rainbow Mountain

---

58 ✦ **YOU CHOOSE!**

---

60 ✦ Show-Off Map
62 ✦ Quiz Answers
63 ✦ Glossary
64 ✦ Index

Red rock rules!

Look up any tricky words in the glossary at the back of the book.

MEET THE SHOW-OFFS

Our **PLANET** is a bit like its **PEOPLE** – it just can't help **SHOWING OFF** from time to time. We've all done it – maybe by trying to **IMPRESS** our friends by attempting to be fast, funny, clever or super skilful. So how does **EARTH** show off?

Well, it's a **BIG** place with thousands of different **LANDSCAPES** and all kinds of **AWESOME FEATURES** across every continent. It's these **NATURAL WONDERS OF THE WORLD** that are showcased in this book.

Anywhere less... stingy?

PRESENTING...

- Towering mountains
- Powerful glaciers
- Colossal icebergs
- Stupendous waves
- Strange lakes
- Mighty rivers
- Booming waterfalls
- Epic volcanoes
- Deep, deep canyons
- Astonishing caves
- Giant craters
- Incredible rainforests
- Vast deserts
- Curious islands

And much, MUCH more!

CHOOSE YOUR SHOW-OFF JOURNEY!

There are four sections, grouping Earth's most stunning natural wonders together:

This doesn't feel volcano-proof to me.

HIGH AND MIGHTY
mountains, volcanoes, cliffs, glaciers and icebergs

WET AND WILD
seas, lakes, rivers, waterfalls, hot springs and surf

DEEP AND DANGEROUS
canyons, caves, craters and valleys

VAST AND VARIED
deserts, forests, salt flats and sand dunes

In each section you'll find facts, figures, wildlife, legends, and true stories of remarkable things that people have done in these places. There are also Top Five lists, battles between wonders and mini-quizzes.

Time to start EXPLORING!

✦ 1 ✦
HIGH AND MIGHTY

Let's meet some of the planet's most EPIC natural features – things so HUGE, they can't help but show themselves off!

If you're a big, beautiful planet like Earth, then you're going to be home to all kinds of awesome places: **MASSIVE MOUNTAINS**, **VIOLENT VOLCANOES**, **GIANT GLACIERS**, **INCREDIBLE ICEBERGS** and many other simply **ENORMOUS** things. Let's meet some of them...

Are you CERTAIN we left the car up here?

1. It's the HIGHEST POINT ON EARTH, but how long does it take to climb: **40 hours** or **40 days**?

2. This rosy rock is SPECIAL for all kinds of reasons, but what makes it red: **iron** or **fossils**?

3. This GIANT GLACIER is old and slow, and was once damaged by what: **bombs** or **forest fires**?

4. This spectacular African mountain is HOT and DRY at the bottom, but what's it like at the top: **hot and wet** or **cold and smelly**?

5. This MONSTER volcano on a famous island in the Pacific Ocean is partly what: **underwater** or **hollow**?

6. This RUMBLING, VIOLENT volcano suddenly appeared where one night: **in a cornfield** or **in a car park**?

7. It's a BIG BAD volcano with a long history of eruptions, but which people did it bury under tonnes of ASH: **Vikings** or **Romans**?

8. These are beautiful, curved MOUNTAINS OF VIVID RED SAND, but what's the quickest way to get down them: **ski** or **roll**?

9. These amazing SPIKY PEAKS are home to the world's longest what: **tunnel** or **staircase**?

Answers on page 62

Read on to find out if you guessed right, and to really get to know these giant SHOW-OFFS...

MOUNT EVEREST

This is the BIG ONE, a real show-off – and why not? It's the highest point on Earth! Everest is a terrifying beast of frozen rock over 8 km high, but because it's the BIGGEST, lots of people want to take on the challenge of climbing to the top...

How did it get so mahoosive?
Everest is basically a giant CRASH SITE. Two sections of Earth's surface, called tectonic plates, are slowly moving towards each other. Where they meet, the rock is forced upwards, forming the Himalayan Mountains, including Everest. And it's still rising by about 4 mm a year!

Climbing the Big E
Attempting to climb the highest mountain on the planet is a SCARY CHALLENGE. The main problem is that air contains less oxygen the higher you go, so it's very hard to breathe. Most climbers carry heavy tanks of oxygen with them.

Here are some other challenges to overcome:

- ◆ You have to spend MONTHS on the mountain to get used to the thin air before even starting
- ◆ You have to WEAR LOTS of SPECIAL EQUIPMENT
- ◆ You have to be TRAINED by an expert local guide – often one of the Sherpa people who have lived in these mountains for centuries
- ◆ You need to be FIT and STRONG
- ◆ The climb takes 40 days. Yes, FORTY!
- ◆ You have to turn back if the weather gets bad (and on Everest, we're talking EXTREME wind and snow)

Peak poo

There is a LOT of poo on Everest! Why? Because there are no toilets on the mountain and hundreds of people climb it each year. Poo doesn't decompose in the freezing temperatures; it just stays there hard and frozen. These days, climbers take their own waste off the mountain, so don't forget those tie-up bags…

◆ VITAL FACTS ◆

Where? In the Himalayan Mountains between Tibet (part of China) and Nepal

How big? A staggering 8,848.86 m (10 times taller than the highest skyscraper)

What else is it called? Chomolungma (Tibetan), Sagarmatha (Nepali)

How dangerous? Over 300 people have died on Mount Everest

Why am I doing this? HELP!

Gear needed:

1. Thermal suit
2. Gloves plus big mittens
3. Special boots with crampons
4. Poles
5. Climbing harness
6. Ice axe
7. Breathing mask
8. Lots of layers of clothes
9. Sleeping bag
10. Ski goggles
11. Pee bottle*
12. Water bottle
13. Helmet
14. Head torch

*where did you think you were going to pee?

A short trip

In 2007 a man called Wim Hof climbed 7,400 m up Everest wearing SHORTS and SANDALS. This is most definitely NOT recommended!

ULURU

In the remote, baking-hot centre of Australia is what looks like a COLOSSAL, half-buried, sleeping red elephant. This isn't just a giant rock, it's a sacred place that glows when the Sun is low in the sky. Welcome to Uluru.

◆ VITAL FACTS ◆

How big? 3.6 km long

How high? 348 m (taller than the Eiffel Tower in Paris)

Once called? Ayers Rock

Why red? The rock is full of iron

How old? 550 million years (that's VERY old, in case you're not sure)

The Dreaming

Uluru is not just a stunning landmark. It is a significant site for indigenous people who have lived in the area for over 60,000 years. The rock holds spiritual importance for the local Anangu people, and ownership was returned to them by the Australian government in 1985. They act as guides today, telling stories about the Dreaming – a time when they believe the world was created by great serpents and other beings.

Not for climbing

People are no longer allowed to climb Uluru because the local people regard the rock as a sacred place that shouldn't be walked upon.

No, I don't sell ice cream.

Visit – but watch out!

250,000 people visit this World Heritage Site each year, but they need be careful…

- ◆ It gets very hot in the daytime
- ◆ The local flies LOVE annoying humans
- ◆ There are snakes about (as well as kangaroos, emus, camels and more)

A curse?

There are many stories about visitors who took stones from Uluru as souvenirs but then suffered bad luck. Some local people believe that misfortune will befall anyone who climbs the rock, such as the three tourists who got trapped in a steep crevice and had to be rescued by helicopter in 2016. Is there really a curse? YOU DECIDE.

✦ VITAL FACTS ✦

How long? 30 km
How wide? 5 km
How thick? 170 m
How fast? It crawls at about 2 m a day
How old? 18,000 years

PERITO MORENO GLACIER

Near the tip of South America, in the great Andes Mountains, a vast, creaking ICE MONSTER is sliding into a huge lake with unstoppable force. This is a glacier, and with the power to grind away mountains as it moves, it's one of the most mind-boggling sights on Earth.

Erm, exactly what IS a glacier?

A glacier is a huge, slow-moving river of ice and snow. It forms when new snow falls in the mountains and presses down on the old snow underneath, compacting it into ice. Pulled by gravity, the ice slides from the mountains into the valleys, forming a million-tonne glacier.

Something funny must be going on – I'm cracking up!

KABOOM!

As well as the creaking of the moving ice and gigantic splashes as it breaks up, the Perito Moreno glacier has caused even bigger noises:

- ✦ Every few years, water builds up on one side of the glacier until eventually it smashes the ice apart with a mega explosion of sound and a crashing wave of freezing water. This is called a rupture.

- ✦ To try to stop the rupture flooding nearby farmland, in 1939 the Argentine Navy bombed the glacier to give the water another way to flow!

Risky treks

Each year a few tourists are brave enough to trek across the ice, led by expert guides. Why is this risky? Because glaciers are covered in NASTY giant cracks called crevasses, sometimes over 30 m deep. Since ice is VERY slippery, that's a COLD bye-bye if you fall in...

TOP FIVE!

Colossal Cliffs

One of the most IMPRESSIVE (and scariest) sights in the world is a steep ROCK FACE, plunging into the sea, battered by wind or waves. There are also TOWERING cliffs in valleys and on mountainsides, some with INCREDIBLE WATERFALLS tumbling off the edge. Here are five of the most WONDROUS!

✦ 5 ✦
WHITE CLIFFS OF DOVER
(UK)

These 100-m-high, white-chalk cliffs are so bright, they can be seen from France on clear days! Amazingly they were once part of the SEA FLOOR!

The rock is made from skeletons of tiny creatures that sank to the seabed millions of years ago. As the land changed over time, the rocks lifted up and became cliffs. They wear away by 20–30 cm every year, bashed by winter storms. Strange things are sometimes revealed, including ancient shark teeth.

✦ 4 ✦
CLIFFS OF MOHER
(Ireland)

The west coast of Ireland faces the mighty Atlantic Ocean, so these 200-m-high cliffs are regularly battered by big bully waves.

Visitors can walk along a SCARY PATH close to the edge, running for over 8 km. As well as a magnificent view, visitors can see thousands of birds, including puffins and razorbills, nesting on tiny ledges up high. The cliffs also feature in one of the Harry Potter™ films.

"I'm not waving – my hand's stuck!"

"Quick, take a photo!"

"Welcome to my cliffs. Now go home."

✦ 3 ✦
EL CAPITAN
(USA)

If you like your cliffs BAD and BOLD, then this big daddy of a rock face in California is for you. It's 900 m high, almost VERTICAL and one of the SCARIEST CLIMBS ever.

Climbing one of the trickiest parts (called The Nose – really!) can take a whole day and is only for experts such as Alex Honnold, who reached the top without any ropes. Do not try this at home. True, it's UNLIKELY you've got a 900-m cliff at home...

✦ 2 ✦
KJERAG
(Norway)

This mountain takes 10 hours to walk to the top, where it plunges 1,084 m down to a fjord (a narrow body of water between cliffs). It's simply BREATHTAKING. Local people say that Kjerag has its own mysterious sound – an occasional cracking boom. CREEPY!

There's also a giant crack in the cliff face nearby where a massive boulder has been wedged for 50,000 years. Visitors stand on this rock to have their photo taken, and it's so popular you usually have to QUEUE.

✦ 1 ✦
DRAKENSBERG
(South Africa)

These MONSTER cliffs are over 1,000 m, and are so high that their tops are often above the clouds. They form a dramatic curved wall of rock called The Amphitheatre. A waterfall tumbles over the edge, dropping 947 m (that's 10 TIMES higher than the Statue of Liberty in New York City – woah).

The name Drakensberg is an Afrikaans word meaning 'Dragon Mountains', and nearby eerie caves contain ancient rock art. The mountain is also home to VULTURES and BABOONS. Impressive!

MOUNT KILIMANJARO

Most gigantic mountains stand between other massive peaks in mountain ranges, but Kilimanjaro is different. It stands alone, soaring above the Tanzanian plains. Thousands of people attempt to climb it every year but around half have to turn back, ZONKED by the lack of oxygen once higher than 4,000 m.

◆ VITAL FACTS ◆

How high? 5,895 m

Where is it? Tanzania

When did this dormant volcano last erupt? About 200,000 years ago

How long does it take to climb? 6–7 days

How does it smell? Volcanic gas makes it smell eggy at the top. YUCK!

FACTIMANJARO

◆ It can be a sizzling 30°C at the base and -5°C at the summit! How do you dress for THAT?

◆ The ice on the mountaintop is disappearing due to climate change and could be GONE by 2050

◆ In 2014, a CRICKET MATCH was played on the flat crater at the top!

I am NOT getting that!

Are there REALLY elephants on the mountain?

No. Elephants, giraffes and cape buffaloes live on the grassy plains around Kilimanjaro. However, climbers sometimes see warthogs, dik-diks, chameleons and mongooses on the lower parts of the mountain.

◆ Records for climbing the BIG K ◆

Oldest person: Anne Lorimor – 89 years old

Youngest person: Ognjen Živković – 5 years old

Fastest person (running): Karl Egloff – 4 hours, 56 mins

Fastest wheelchair ascent: Bernard Goosen – 6 days

✦ VITAL FACTS ✦

How high? 4,205 m (above sea level)

Which country is it in? USA

When did it last erupt? Around 4,500 years ago

What is on top? 13 giant telescopes – and snow in winter!

Can it be climbed? Yes, but there's also a road to drive to the top

MAUNA KEA

Some people say this inactive Hawaiian volcano is really the tallest mountain on Earth. That's because most of it's under the Pacific Ocean, and from its base on the seabed Mauna Kea measures an epic 10,211 m! Is that a fair way to look at it, or a bit CHEEKY?

Why are there telescopes on the mountain?

Sensible question. Well, because Mauna Kea is so dry and high, it's ideal for OBSERVING SPACE. A number of large observatories have been built here since the 1960s for scientific research. It's a CHAMPION place to stargaze!

I told you it's not a café!

Heavy fact!

Mauna Kea is so TOTALLY MASSIVE that it's being SQUASHED by its own weight! The mountain is very gradually flattening, and loses a teeny-tiny bit of height each year. Well, actually, about 1 mm every six years, so not exactly a BIG DIFFERENCE, eh?

Me big! *Me bigger!*

Some mountains just STAND THERE doing ZILCH for thousands of years, while others go KABOOM! Get ready to meet two of the world's most active (and dangerous) show-offs!

THE BATTLE

In the left corner:
PARÍCUTIN
Fiery new kid on the block

Life's a BLAST!

Why is Parícutin SPECTACULAR?

◆ This volcano didn't even exist 100 years ago!

◆ It suddenly emerged from a farmer's cornfield in Mexico in 1943

◆ Within a week it was 150 m high

◆ It poured out red-hot lava, swallowing two towns and spitting ash and volcanic bombs for nine years

SHOW-OFF RATING
◆ SIZE **6**
◆ EXPLOSIVE power **8**
◆ DANGER rating **7**

A volcano is born

In the small Mexican town of Parícutin, people were amazed to hear VIOLENT RUMBLING and see a black hill suddenly grow out of the ground, spewing hot smoke and gas. They watched it spit BURNING ORANGE into the night sky. As hot ash began to pour outwards, farms and houses were engulfed by the new volcano's surging growth. The town is now gone, but tourists visit the site to see the half-buried church of San Juan.

OF THE VOLCANOES

Get outta my way!

In the right corner:
VESUVIUS
Old-school rowdy Roman-basher

Why is Vesuvius SPECTACULAR?

✦ This volcano in Italy is big and bad

✦ It famously went BOOM in AD 79, blasting four towns

✦ Vesuvius buried the cities of Pompeii and Herculaneum under ash and mud

✦ It's still active and last erupted in 1944, pouring out vast amounts of lava

Run, Romans, run!

If you were a Roman living in Pompeii in AD 79, you had two choices. You could either stay and watch the spectacular sight of nearby Mount Vesuvius erupting (and hope that your house wasn't bashed) or you could RUN FOR YOUR LIFE. Stones, ash and gases were blasted an incredible 33 km into the sky, before raining down on to the city. Pompeii ended up buried under a huge layer of ash. Vesuvius is STILL ACTIVE and has erupted about 35 times since then!

SHOW-OFF RATING

✦ SIZE **8**

✦ EXPLOSIVE power **9**

✦ DANGER rating **10**

SOSSUSVLEI SAND DUNES

In the hot Namib Desert is a white salt lake, dry and flat, surrounded by EPIC fiery-red sand dunes the size of small mountains. This is Sossusvlei, one of the driest places in the world and a favourite destination for sand boarders who zip down the dunes for extreme fun.

✦ VITAL FACTS ✦

How big are the dunes? Massive. The tallest is 388 m

Can you climb them? Yes, but it's very slow and hard going because of the soft sand

How long does it take? A 170-m dune takes 45 minutes to climb

Why are they so red? The sand is full of rust-coloured iron

Do the dunes move? Yes, the wind forms them and changes them gradually

Sand dune creation

Here's where they come from:
- ◆ The sand comes from the rocks in hills that have been WORN AWAY by rivers
- ◆ The tiny particles flow down into the sea, then are WASHED UP on beaches
- ◆ Strong winds BLOW the sand inland
- ◆ Obstacles like rocks trap the sand and it PILES UP as the wind blows, slowly growing until a dune forms

Drinks are on me!

Clever beetle

It's VERY tough for animals to survive in a hot, dry wilderness, but the crafty Namib Desert beetle collects water from morning fog using special bumps on its back.

Who needs snow to ski?

Henrik May doesn't! In 2010 he set a world record for the fastest SAND SKIING ever at Sossusvlei. He HURTLED down one of the giant dunes at 92 kph.

VITAL FACTS

Where? In the Alps of northern Italy

How big? The highest mountain is 3,343 m

Famous for? Skiing, mountain climbing and extreme sports

Watch out for... Avalanches and blizzards

DOLOMITES

It's usually a BAD IDEA to jump off a jagged 3,000-m-high mountain wearing a parachute, but people do it for FUN in the Dolomite Mountains! This majestic range of fairy-tale peaks is home to hairy zigzag roads, giant tunnels and an ancient iceman.

Wheeeeeee!

BASE jumpers like to HURL THEMSELVES off these rock faces, which are some of the highest in Europe. It's a dangerous sport involving a short freefall and then a slower parachute descent into a valley below. Some BASE jumpers wear wingsuits so they can stay in the air for longer by gliding.

I want wings!

OK, who's this iceman dude, then?

In 1991, two hikers stumbled across the MUMMIFIED BODY of a man over 5,000 years old, preserved by ice high in the mountains. Scientists named him Otzi the Iceman. He had tattoos, a beard and a copper axe, and was wearing a woven-grass cloak and bearskin hat. Otzi was probably a warrior – he even had an arrowhead buried in his shoulder!

Nip upstairs for me would you, dearest?

If you live in Valstagna in the Dolomites and want to visit your bestie in nearby Asiago, then you face Calà del Sasso, THE WORLD'S LONGEST OPEN STAIRCASE!

- It has 4,444 steps
- It is a climb of 744 m
- It is over 600 years old
- It takes 2+ hours to climb
- It is mega slippery when wet

✦ 2 ✦
WET AND WILD

WATER has played a huge part in creating some of the world's most awesome places. MIND-BLOWING amounts of it swirl around the planet every day, sometimes surging with UNSTOPPABLE POWER, and other times sculpting weird shapes and creating majestic colours.

*From **GIANT RIVERS** with **RAGING WATERFALLS** and **MONSTER WAVES** smashing into the shore, to **EERIE LAKES** and **VAST CORAL REEFS** – it's time to take you on a tour that is pure **WOW**.*

Nice day for a dip!

1. This place has SERIOUSLY GIANT WAVES, but where is it: **Switzerland** or **Portugal**?

2. It's a VAST FROZEN LAKE, but what do people play on it: **ice golf** or **ice karate**?

3. This is a truly GIANT LIVING THING, but is it made of: **skeletons** or **poo**?

4. This is a MASSIVE RIVER that is home to what: **pink dolphins** or **orange whales**?

5. This is an INCREDIBLY LONG RIVER, but does it flow: **south to north** or **north to south**?

6. It's the WORLD'S LARGEST WATERFALL. Does it fall into: **Dracula's Armpit** or **the Devil's Throat**?

7. It's the LOWEST POINT ON EARTH, but what is it full of: **salt** or **pepper**?

8. This SCI-FI LANDSCAPE of hot ponds has a name that means what: **cotton castle** or **velvet volcano**?

9. What makes this lake in Australia PINK? **flamingos** or **tiny microbes**?

Answers on page 62

Read on to find out if you guessed right, and to really get to know these raging SHOW-OFFS...

NAZARÉ SURF

Surfers have long debated where has the biggest waves on the planet. Well, argument over – it's here! The small coastal town of Nazaré in Portugal not only faces the might of the vast Atlantic Ocean, but is also at the end of a giant underwater valley that channels water into monster waves.

◆ VITAL FACTS ◆

How high are these waves? Some are over 30 m (taller than a beech tree)

Where are they formed? Up to 210 km out at sea

What makes them so big? A deep underwater canyon and strong winds blowing inland

Are they easy to surf? What??? NO WAY! They are incredibly difficult to surf

Nazaré surf DOs and DON'Ts

 DO
Learn to swim first

 **DON'T**
Wear a top hat

 DO
Spend years practising on smaller waves

DON'T
Surf on a bin lid

 DO
Study how the experts do it

DON'T
Take your pet labradoodle

I think I'll go back to playing chess!

How do you surf these beasts?

Only a very few brave people take it on:

- ◆ Top PROFESSIONAL surfers are the only ones who should tackle the biggest waves
- ◆ It's impossible to paddle against the surf's force – surfers are TOWED OUT by special JET SKIS
- ◆ The power of the water is so great that injuries are common – OUCH is heard a lot!
- ◆ The record is held by Sebastian Steudtner who surfed a wave of 26.2 m in 2020

LAKE BAIKAL

✦ VITAL FACTS ✦

How big is it? 636 km long and 79 km wide

How deep? 1,642 m (the world's two tallest buildings would disappear into it, one on top of the other...)

Where is it? Siberia in Russia

How long does it freeze for? About four months each winter

Where does the water come from? The lake is fed by over 330 rivers!

Welcome to the world's deepest and possibly strangest lake. It's so ENORMOUS that it contains one-fifth of the world's fresh water, and its surface is larger than Belgium. But Lake Baikal is also remote and extremely COLD in winter, so very few people live on its shores.

Can trucks really drive across it?

Yes! In winter the ice is often over 1 m thick, strong enough to support vehicles. In fact, a special ICE ROAD is opened each year to allow people to drive to one of the lake's large islands. Do NOT try this with your bike on a local pond.

ULTRA relaxed!

Not panicking AT ALL!

YOU can get that ball – it's 11 km away!

Wacky winter sports

Lake Baikal hosts all of these:

✦ ICE YACHTING ✦

✦ DOG SLEDDING ✦

✦ ICE GOLF ✦

✦ TUBE RIDING ✦

✦ CAMPING IN YURTS ON THE ICE ✦

✦ ICE SPEEDWAY ✦

GREAT BARRIER REEF

The Great Barrier Reef is the LARGEST LIVING STRUCTURE ON EARTH. It's a magical marine environment made of coral — the hard skeletons of billions of tiny living organisms called polyps. It's also home to an ENORMOUS variety of sea creatures. It's just totally AWESOME.

Yes, I am a nudibranch. Stop giggling!

Tee-hee, NUDEY-branch!

Wait a minute... WHAT is a NUDIBRANCH?

A nudibranch is a type of brightly coloured sea slug. Its name means 'naked gills'.

A selection of reef wildlife
- Sea turtles
- Dugongs
- Clownfish
- Humpback whales
- Giant clams
- Seahorses
- Nudibranchs
- Sea snakes
- Sharks

There must be a LOT of polyps in the Great Barrier Reef, right?

Are you KIDDING? There's up to 10,000 polyps in ONE SQUARE METRE of coral. Multiply that by a reef 2.3 million metres long... there isn't space on this page for all the ZEROS!

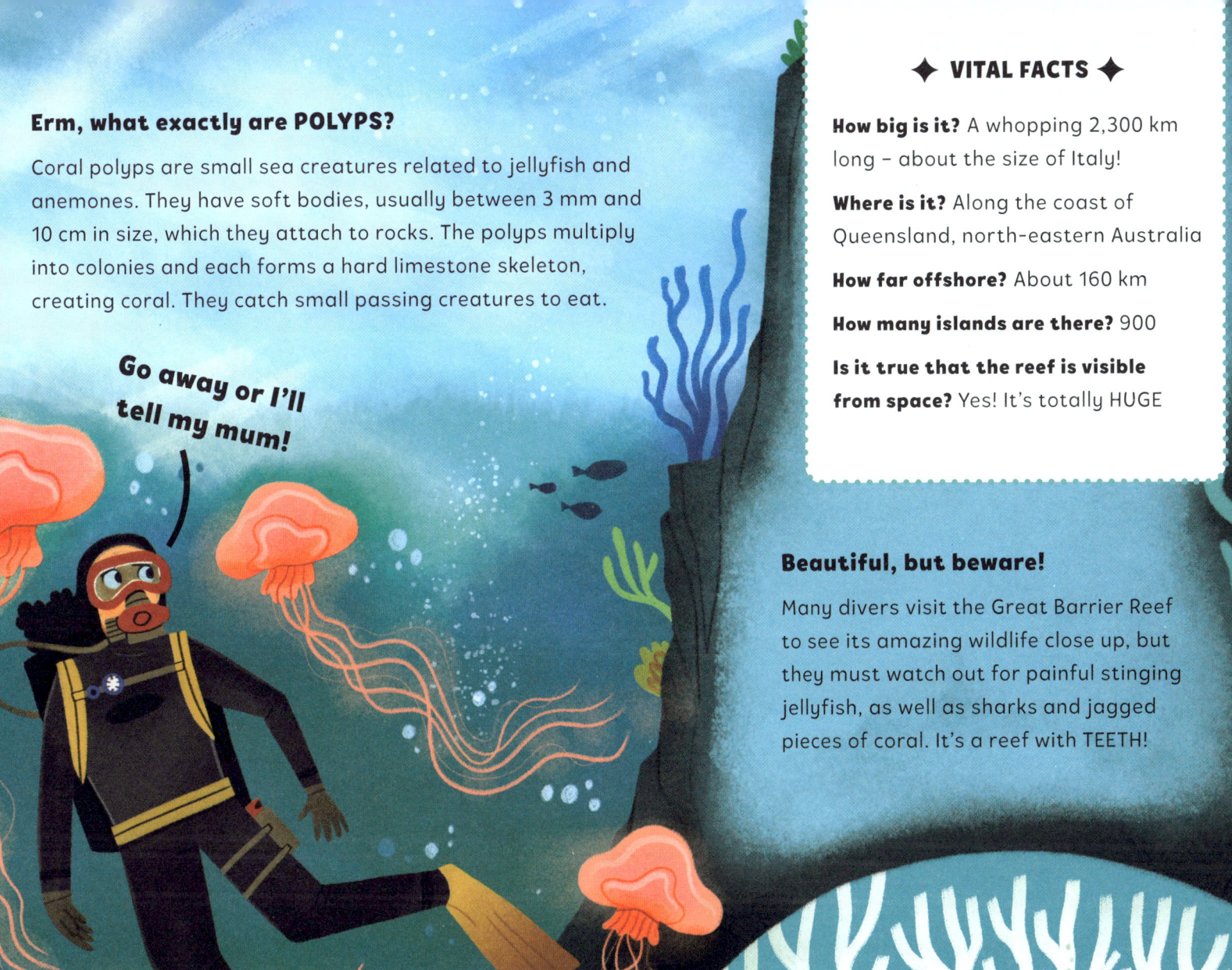

Erm, what exactly are POLYPS?

Coral polyps are small sea creatures related to jellyfish and anemones. They have soft bodies, usually between 3 mm and 10 cm in size, which they attach to rocks. The polyps multiply into colonies and each forms a hard limestone skeleton, creating coral. They catch small passing creatures to eat.

Go away or I'll tell my mum!

◆ VITAL FACTS ◆

How big is it? A whopping 2,300 km long – about the size of Italy!

Where is it? Along the coast of Queensland, north-eastern Australia

How far offshore? About 160 km

How many islands are there? 900

Is it true that the reef is visible from space? Yes! It's totally HUGE

Beautiful, but beware!

Many divers visit the Great Barrier Reef to see its amazing wildlife close up, but they must watch out for painful stinging jellyfish, as well as sharks and jagged pieces of coral. It's a reef with TEETH!

Why are coral reefs so colourful?

Good question. The polyps themselves have no colour, but their bodies contain algae of many different colours. Now you know!

Sadly, this wonderful sea environment faces a lot of problems:

1. Climate change is causing some of the coral to lose its colour and die (this is called bleaching)

2. Pollution, tourism and overfishing all have a negative effect on the reef

3. Outbreaks of a polyp-munching beast called the **crown of thorns starfish** have destroyed large areas of coral – these starfish can be over 30 cm across, with 21 arms and venomous spines

There are small rivers, big rivers, huge rivers, and then TWO GIANTS. Imagine a river so long, it would take 66 days to swim. Or one so wide, no bridges can reach across. Welcome to the Amazon and the Nile! But which is the GREATEST?

THE BATTLE

In the left corner:
AMAZON
South American titan

Why is the Amazon so INCREDIBLE?

- It's the biggest river on the planet by far (14 km wide in places)
- It carries about one-fifth of all the fresh water on Earth!
- Enough water flows out of it to fill 87 Olympic-sized swimming pools every SECOND!
- It's 100 m deep in places

SHOW-OFF RATING
- SIZE 10
- IMPORTANCE 9
- Water POWER 10

The Lord of the Jungle

The Amazon River begins high in the Andes Mountains of Peru. It then flows for a STONKING 6,500 km through Brazil's vast Amazon rainforest before it empties gigantic quantities of muddy water into the Atlantic Ocean. Over 1,100 tributary rivers pour into the Amazon from 10 different countries. Each year it floods an area of forest the size of England!

OF THE MIGHTY RIVERS

In the right corner:
NILE
African hero

HUGE HIPPOS in here!

Why is the Nile such a SPECIAL river?

- It's the longest river on the planet (probably!)
- Millions of people across Africa depend on it for water
- It allowed the great civilization of ancient Egypt to become powerful
- It's so epic that 10 percent of all rain that falls on Africa drains into the Nile

The Gift of Africa

It's very hard to measure the length of a river, especially one as EPIC as the Nile, but most experts agree that this is the longest river on the planet. This wondrous waterway changed history. Around 4,000 years ago, its floods helped turn scorching desert into FERTILE FARMLAND where Egyptians could grow enough food to eat and sell. As the Nile flows from south to north, water from 11 African countries feeds into it. Some nations have even built dams to generate electricity. It's pure POWER!

SHOW-OFF RATING
- SIZE **9**
- IMPORTANCE **10**
- Water POWER **7**

IGUAZU FALLS

As you approach, there is a RUMBLING, then a deep ROARING and finally a BOOMING CRASH. Your face is soaked by spray as you see the astonishing might of Iguazu, the largest system of waterfalls on Earth!

◆ VITAL FACTS ◆

How big are the falls? Water drops over an edge 2,700 m wide

Where is it? On the border between Argentina and Brazil

How high are the falls? Between 60 and 82 m

How many falls are there? Usually 275, but if it rains a lot, 300!

How much water flows? Up to 14 million litres a SECOND

Why is it so, well, SPECTACULAR?

The huge Iguazu River drops over a ledge of hard basalt rock, wearing away the softer rock below and forming a terrifying NATURAL CHASM called the Devil's Throat. The sound of the water is VERY LOUD and it also creates multiple RAINBOWS.

How can I see this wonder?

The falls have so many visitors (over 1.5 million a year) that they have their own airport! There are various ways to see the water:

- ◆ Viewing platforms
- ◆ Walkways
- ◆ Helicopter rides
- ◆ Inflatable boats that take you under the spray (you'll get SOAKED)

A wild place

Iguazu Falls is surrounded by rainforest and lots of wild animals, including monkeys, toucans, alligators, jaguars and butterflies. But watch out for coatis, small aggressive mammals that bite and have learned to steal from tourists' bags.

At last I can afford a decent holiday...

✦ VITAL FACTS ✦

How big is it? About 80 km long and 18 km wide

Is it deep? Yes, 304 m, which is about the height of the Shard building in London

How much salt is in it? The water is 34 percent salt, about 10 times saltier than the ocean!

Can you really float in it? You sure can! The very salty water is denser than our bodies

Which country is it in? It's located between Israel and Jordan

DEAD SEA

The Dead Sea is actually a lake, and it's rather special. Situated 430 m below sea level, it's the LOWEST POINT on Earth's surface. Why DEAD? Because it's so salty that animals and plants can't survive in the water – so don't try FISHING!

Why do so many people visit the lake?

For centuries, people have visited the Dead Sea because they believe that MINERALS found in the water (and in the mud at the bottom) are good for the skin and can ease health conditions. Plus it's FUN to float in the water. It's, well, DEAD GOOD!

Now I just need some floating coffee...

Dead Sea fact selection

✦ You can swim in the water but it STINGS your eyes and mouth

✦ The lake turned RED in 1980 due to algae that multiplied when the water was less salty.

✦ Huge LUMPS of SALT form around the shore

The vanishing sea

The lake is actually shrinking each year – this is partly because high temperatures cause the water to evaporate. Shockingly, the Dead Sea could even disappear in the next 100 years... EEK!

Dead sells!

All these products can be bought online:

✦ Dead Sea foot cream
✦ Dead Sea mud face-mask
✦ Dead Sea bath salts
✦ Dead Sea shampoo

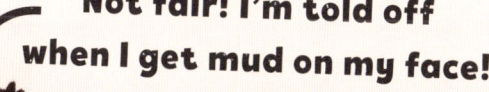

Not fair! I'm told off when I get mud on my face!

PAMUKKALE

Some places on Earth have magical FAIRY-TALE qualities, and Pamukkale in Turkey is one of them. The name means 'cotton castle' and it describes the strange ZINGING WHITE limestone formations and shallow pools. Some of these pools are HOT, fed by underground volcanic springs. Incredible.

✦ VITAL FACTS ✦

How many hot springs are there? 17 spread over a large area

Is the water really hot? Some of it is nearly boiling (100°C), some at bath temperature (35°C)

Are the pools human-made? No, they are entirely natural

What else is here? The ancient Greeks built a city called Hierapolis at the top of the hill, but it was destroyed by an earthquake, leaving only ruins and a MASSIVE open-air theatre

What exactly is the white stuff?

Good question. The hot water from the springs contains a dissolved mineral called CALCIUM CARBONATE. As the water evaporates, this mineral is left behind and becomes a hard white limestone rock called TRAVERTINE.

Where's the thermal water slide?

Explain THERMAL POOLS – please!

OK, since you asked nicely:

1. Deep underground are huge amounts of hot rock and magma (molten rocks)
2. Rainwater seeping into the ground is heated by the geothermal energy from these rocks
3. Some of the water comes out of the ground as hot springs
4. It flows into the flat travertine terraces, leaving hot/warm (thermal) pools

Things NOT to do in Pamukkale thermal pools

✦ Drop in some teabags to make a brew
✦ Do your washing up
✦ Launch your giant inflatable unicorn...

◆ VITAL FACTS ◆

How big is this pinkie? 600 m long and 250 m wide, so not huge

Where is it exactly? On a small island called Middle Island near the south-west coast of Australia

Can I swim in it, and will I turn pink? It's hard to get to (there are no roads) but people have swum in it and not turned into flamingos!

What kind of lake is it? It's a salt lake, like the Dead Sea, but not as salty. And we can't use the salt because it's toxic. Yikes!

LAKE HILLIER

What? What! WHAATT!! There's a lake that's entirely PINK? Yes, Lake Hillier in Southwest Australia looks like a GIANT has squashed some BUBBLEGUM. Why is it pink? Well, this fascinating mystery has puzzled scientists for decades...

I'm wild about pink

There are no fish in the lake, but wildlife in the forests around it includes:

- ◆ Wallabies
- ◆ Bush rats
- ◆ Crowned snakes
- ◆ 31 types of birds

Marooned!

Lake Hillier is named after a sailor whose ship visited the island in 1803. In 1826, some other English sailors ANNOYED their captain so much that he cast them ashore on the island and sailed off! Were they MAROONED or PINKED? Ha, ha!

Don't leave me!

OK, I'll stay a while.

So why is it pink?

This has been a mystery that would fox even SHERLOCK HOLMES, but some clever scientists have studied water samples and found the answer. Lake Hillier contains a mix of salt-loving microbes that produce a red colour – a kind of living dye!

✦ 3 ✦
DEEP AND DANGEROUS

Earth has LOTS of holes. Some of them are teeny-weeny, some are, well, A BIT DULL, some are deep and some are big. Some are VERY BIG. A few are AWESOME – and it's the deep, dangerous show-off chasms you'll discover in these pages.

Welcome to **GIANT RIVER GORGES** a **MILE DEEP** and **VAST, MYSTERIOUS CAVES**. Discover **WILD DESERT VALLEYS** and a **HUGE CRATER** blasted into existence by a **MASSIVE METEOR** – it's time to explore!

1. It's an ENORMOUS, DEEP gorge, but how did someone jump across it: **by motorbike** or **catapult**?

2. What's at the bottom of this HUGE HOLE: **an underground river** or **a hot mud lake**?

3. What happened to the vast IRON LUMP from space that made this epic crater? Was it: **burned up on impact** or **sold for scrap metal**?

4. Some of these MASSIVE STONE COLUMNS are as tall as what: **Mount Fuji** or **the Eiffel Tower**?

5. What was found at the bottom of the deepest part of the ocean: **a plastic bag** or **pirate treasure**?

6. Iceland is famous for its amazing volcanic features, but what brings this gushing Icelandic geyser to life: **earthquakes** or **tomatoes**?

7. This booming geyser in New Zealand is spectacular, but what makes it pong of rotten eggs: **people cooking their breakfast in the hot water** or **sulphur**?

Answers on page 62

Read on to find out if you guessed right, and to really get to know these SHOW-OFF holes...

GRAND CANYON

A canyon is a deep, rocky valley with steep sides. Canyons are often big, but to see a MONSTER one, you need to travel to Arizona, USA. Here you will find a truly colossal hole in the desert called the Grand Canyon!

How does a river make a gorge that big?

The fast-flowing Colorado River has been winding over high rocky ground for over 6 MILLION YEARS. In that time, it has worn away the rocks to make a deep channel called a canyon. Water can be TOUGH!

No, you can't go for a paddle!

Walk into the sky...

FIVE MILLION tourists come each year to stand and STARE at the amazing view from the edge of the canyon. Some of them are brave enough to step out for an even better view along the SKYWALK – a viewing bridge with a glass floor above a BIG drop...

Hand over the crisps and no one gets hurt!

Bish, bash, bosh – watch out!

There are some DANGEROUS WILD ANIMALS around the Grand Canyon, including bears, rattlesnakes, scorpions and mountain lions. But the one that attacks people most often is... a SQUIRREL! Yes, the small rock squirrel is known to jump on visitors to steal their picnics!

> ✦ **VITAL FACTS** ✦
>
> **How big is it?** 446 km long and up to 29 km wide
>
> **How deep?** 1,830 m deep in places
>
> **What made such a mahoosive hole?** The Colorado River, mostly
>
> **Does anyone live in the Grand Canyon?** For thousands of years, native American tribes lived around the canyon, and some still have towns and land there today

A show-off place attracts show-off people!

Being so HUGE and famous, the Grand Canyon attracts lots of people who do VERY risky stunts:

✦ In 1914, two men drove a tiny CAR down the mega-steep sides of the canyon and back up again. There were no roads, so they jolted over massive boulders, across streams and through mud flats! At least there were no traffic lights...

Are you sure we go straight on here?

✦ In 1945, a canyon guide called Georgie White jumped in the water with a life jacket and FLOATED 97 km down the river, surviving extra-dangerous fast channels of water called rapids. It took three days altogether! Hopefully she remembered a towel...

✦ In 1999, daredevil rider Robbie Knievel jumped across a narrow part of the canyon on a MOTORBIKE! Well, it saves going the long way round!

Wheeeee!

Yikes, hope I don't need the loo!

✦ In 2013, a stuntman called Nik Wallenda walked across the canyon on a TIGHTROPE. EEK! It took him 23 minutes to cross the 430-m gap. If you are lucky enough to have a canyon in your garden, do NOT try this at home.

PADIRAC CAVE

In south-west France, there is a colossal hole in the ground, a CHASM, that DROPS OVER 100 M DOWN into an amazing cave system. Luckily, the nice owners have built a big staircase and a lift so you can visit this underground WONDERLAND.

✦ VITAL FACTS ✦

How big is it? The giant chasm is only the entrance – in total there are 42 km of caves here!

How deep? 103 m

What else is down there? An underground river, which visitors can travel along by boat, and a turquoise lake

What's in the other caves? Lots of strange rock formations, including a giant 60-m-long stalactite

Can you walk through the caves? Some of the big ones, yes – about 350,000 people visit each year

Who first explored the caves?

In 1889, a French cave enthusiast called Édouard-Alfred Martel set out with some adventurous friends to explore the cave. They used ropes and ladders to climb down, and oil lamps and candles for light. Finding the underground river, they returned the next day with a collapsible canoe. It later capsized, plunging the men into the cold, dark waters (EEK) but they survived and went on exploring for days.

✦ VITAL FACTS ✦

How big is it? About 1,200 m across

How deep? 180 m (it would have once been much deeper – weathering has gradually filled it in)

Where is it? Arizona, USA

Is there really nothing left of the giant meteorite? Some small fragments have been found and can be seen in the museum at the edge of the crater

What was the meteorite made of? Metal – mostly nickel and iron

METEOR CRATER

About 50,000 years ago, there was a VERY big KABOOM in what is now south-west USA. A giant 300,000-tonne METEORITE smashed into the ground, creating an enormous crater over 1.2 km wide. The meteorite vaporized in the heat of this violent impact, but the hole remains and it's IMPRESSIVE.

Tell me more about the kaboom!

Scientists think that the meteorite probably broke off a passing asteroid, hitting the ground at a blistering 41,800 kph. The ENORMOUS PRESSURE and HEAT of the blast caused a shockwave that obliterated everything within several kilometres. About 159 million tonnes of rock blasted into the air. The mammoths around at the time must have had quite a surprise...

Looks like a golf course for giants!

Uh-oh!

Poor Daniel...

A mining engineer called Daniel Barringer bought the crater in 1903 because he was sure that MILLIONS OF TONNES of valuable IRON from the meteorite would be buried inside it. He spent a FORTUNE drilling and digging, but found only tiny fragments. Today the crater is used to train astronauts.

TOP FIVE!

Islands come in all varieties, and NO ONE knows how many there are in the world. Whether you're looking for vast VOLCANOES, beautiful BEACHES or stunning WILDLIFE, here are five of the most AMAZING.

Astonishing Islands

Hi. Come over for dinner!

✦ 5 ✦
KOMODO ISLAND
(Indonesia)

Indonesia is a country made up of an incredible 17,508 islands. One of the most SPECTACULAR is called Komodo. This rocky volcanic island is home to the world's largest lizard, the fearsome KOMODO DRAGON, which grows up to 3 m long. This amazing hunter specializes in ambushing large prey such as deer.

Komodo Island also has a remarkable PINK BEACH, and the coastal waters are home to sharks, huge manta rays and dugongs. Nice.

✦ 4 ✦
LOFOTEN ISLANDS
(Norway)

If you visit the Lofoten Islands off the coast of Norway in June, then you may have trouble sleeping... The islands are inside the ARCTIC CIRCLE, in an area called the 'Land of the Midnight Sun' because the Sun does not set at all during summer. It's also DARK FOR 24 HOURS for most of December!

Visitors come to the seven islands to climb, surf and see the Northern Lights. There's also a DANGEROUS WHIRLPOOL off the coast called the Maelstrom – best to stay RIGHT away from that!

✦ 3 ✦
CLIPPERTON ISLAND
(Pacific Ocean)

Islands don't come much STRANGER than this uninhabited ring-shaped coral atoll. With an EERIE freshwater lagoon at its centre, Clipperton Island is home to the rare masked booby bird, as well as tropical fish and giant crabs.

It also has a CURIOUS HISTORY... visitors include STRANDED SAILORS whose ships were wrecked on the reef, as well as illegal guano (bird poo) miners who sold the STINKY STUFF as fertilizer. Clipperton is nearly 1,000 km from the nearest landmass and hard to get to, so don't plan a visit just yet!

✦ 2 ✦
GALÁPAGOS ISLANDS
(Pacific Ocean)

The only place in the world where you can see a wild Galápagos penguin is a proper SHOW-OFF! The incredible Galápagos Islands are wild, remote and explosive (13 active volcanoes erupt frequently), as well as historic (Darwin's ideas about evolution, erm, evolved here).

But it's the unique WILDLIFE that wows visitors most. Galápagos is home to giant tortoises, alien-like marine iguanas, vampire finches (yes, they drink BLOOD from other birds) and mahoosive whales. EPIC.

✦ 1 ✦
ICELAND
(Iceland)

If you want ICE, it's got the biggest glaciers in Europe. If you want FIRE, it's got 35 active volcanoes. If you want WATER, it's got hundreds of cold fjords, hot springs and gushing geysers. If you want ROCK, it has monster mountains. And if you want to TREMBLE, there are frequent small earthquakes.

But if you want a train, you'll be disappointed – there are no railways. However, there are beautiful white arctic foxes and the occasional polar bear visitor.

ZHANGJIAJIE PILLARS

In the mountains of central China is a strange and enchanting landscape. The SPECTACULAR stone pillars of Zhangjiajie National Forest Park tower over deep wooded ravines, complete with caves, lakes and hanging misty clouds.

◆ VITAL FACTS ◆

How tall are the pillars? Over 40 of them are as tall as the Eiffel Tower (300 m) and one of them is 1,080 m!

How many pillars are there? Over 3,000 in total

What are they made of? Sandstone rock, worn away by the weather over thousands of years

Why do they look familiar? They were the inspiration for the floating mountains in the film *Avatar*

Can weather really wear away hard rock?

Slowly, yes! WIND and RAIN can change the shapes of stone gradually, but if water in the rock also freezes to form ICE, it expands. This breaks away pieces of rock and helps create weird natural structures like these pillars.

How can visitors get a good view of this show-off place?

- ◆ One of the pillars has a GIANT ELEVATOR to the top! It's called the 100 DRAGONS SKY LIFT and is 330 m high!
- ◆ There's also a GLASS BRIDGE across one of the gaps. It's 430 m long with a drop of 300 m below – TOTALLY SCARY!
- ◆ But watch out for sneaky MONKEYS – they love to steal food from tourists.

Race you!

Winging it!

The World Wingsuit Championships are sometimes held in the park – competitors jump off the pillars, aim for targets and land with parachutes. EVEN MORE SCARY!

MARIANA TRENCH

✦ VITAL FACTS ✦

How deep is it? About 11,000 m (it's extremely hard to measure!)

Where is it? In the western Pacific Ocean, near the island of Guam

How big is the trench? Enormous! 2,550 km long and 69 km wide

What is the deepest part called? Challenger Deep, named after the first ship to measure the trench

The DEEPEST, most MYSTERIOUS and LEAST EXPLORED hole isn't on land, but in the ocean: the Mariana Trench. This mighty gash in the Pacific Ocean floor is the deepest point on Earth, and only six people have ever been there. If Mount Everest was placed in these depths, its summit would still be 2 km below the surface of the sea!

What's it like at the bottom?

Very dark and very cold. The greatest problem for human explorers, however, is the enormous PRESSURE caused by the weight of water pressing down. In Challenger Deep, the pressure is 1,000 times greater than at sea level and actually squashes steel diving vessels, so they come up smaller than when they submerged! But amazingly, several kinds of living things can survive even in the deepest seas.

  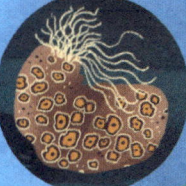

The WiFi here is terrible!

Yeah, but feel the peace, dude!

Things found in the Mariana Trench...

✦ Tiny glowing microorganisms
✦ Shrimp-like creatures
✦ Sea cucumbers
✦ Sea squirts
✦ Mud
✦ Darkness
✦ A plastic bag

Things NOT found in the Mariana Trench...

✦ Pirate treasure
✦ Internet access
✦ Snack bars

Under Earth's surface are hugely POWERFUL FORCES. Deep down, it's so HOT that ROCK MELTS, heating water around it to BOILING POINT. This can burst up out of the ground in a spouting hot spring called a GEYSER. Which of these two famous geysers is the CHAMP?

THE BATTLE

In the left corner:
GEYSIR
Icelandic favourite

Wet and wild!

Why does Geysir sound like GEYSER?

- That's because we get the word *geyser* from the famous hot spring at Geysir in Iceland!
- It's been blasting water up into the air for over 900 years
- The boiling water is usually blasted about 60 m in the air, but it once reached 122 m
- It once erupted every 30 minutes but now it is often dormant for months

SHOW-OFF RATING
- HEIGHT   9
- REGULARITY   3
- POWER   8

Geysir's ups and downs

The Icelandic geyser of Geysir may be renowned, but it's much less active than it used to be. In 1910, it was spouting TWICE AN HOUR but then it stopped altogether six years later. An EARTHQUAKE brought it back to life again, but eruptions were much smaller. To see it erupt now, you have to be VERY LUCKY!

I was 16 when I started waiting to see this!

OF THE GEYSERS

In the right corner:
POHUTU
New Zealand gusher

How rubbish!
Some geysers around the world have been damaged by people throwing litter into them. This blocks the flow of water and can even stop them from erupting.

Hot and stinky!

Why is Pohutu FAMOUS?

✦ It's a very reliable geyser, putting on a show around once an hour

✦ Its steaming gush only reaches about 30 m upwards, but it lasts for 10–20 minutes!

✦ The water is searingly hot: 160–180°C

✦ On the downside, the water contains sulphur, which makes it slightly STINKY

Big splash

The word *pohutu* means 'big splash' in Maori, but the geyser started making a smaller splash when local residents began DRILLING HOLES to use the hot spring water to heat their homes. Which GEEZER thought of THAT?

SHOW-OFF RATING
✦ HEIGHT   7
✦ REGULARITY 10
✦ POWER   6

4
VAST AND VARIED

This section presents a whole range of magnificent natural features from around the world, including one that only appears at certain times and can only be seen in the dark! Here are the unusual, the immense and the mysterious.

Welcome to a **FOREST** so big that it changes **EARTH'S WEATHER**, and an **AWESOME DESERT** that seems to go on forever. Explore **STRANGE LIGHTS** caused by solar storms, a **RAINBOW MOUNTAIN**, **THE WORLD'S BIGGEST MIRROR** – and more!

Why did I bring extra-hot chilli juice?!

1. It's the WORLD'S BIGGEST JUNGLE, but which small insect in it should you avoid at all costs: **bullet ant** or **laser ant**?

2. It's a dynamic NORTHERN LIGHTS SPECTACULAR, but what exactly is producing the glow: **space junk** or **gas**?

3. This is a ghostly white DRY LAKE, but what do visitors here love to do: **take funny photos** or **race e-bikes**?

4. This vast ice sheet is BIGGER THAN A CITY, but what is it made from: **water and dust** or **crystals and chalk**?

5. This is the BOSS of all deserts, but what does its dust help to create around the planet: **orange skies** or **brown clouds**?

6. Here are some of the WEIRDEST ROCK FORMATIONS on the planet, but how were they formed: **cooled lava** or **battling giants**?

7. What was this EXTRAORDINARY STRIPY PEAK hidden by for thousands of years: **moss** or **a glacier**?

Answers on page 62

Read on to find out if you guessed right, and to really get to know these unusual SHOW-OFFS ...

AMAZON RAINFOREST

A wild range of wildlife

The Amazon rainforest is the most biodiverse place on Earth – that means it has more different kinds of living things than anywhere else. The numbers are just MIND-BENDING:

- 378 kinds of reptiles
- 427 types of mammals
- 428 species of amphibians
- 1,294 different birds
- 2,200 varieties of fish
- 40,000 plants
- 2.5 million sorts of insects

And new ones are being found all the time – over 10,000 new beetles have been discovered in just the last 10 years!

This is the BIG DADDY of rainforests, the QUEEN of jungles, the BOSS of tropical trees. It's not just the biggest rainforest on the planet, it's home to the mighty AMAZON RIVER and has more kinds of wildlife than anywhere else on Earth. Respect!

I hate hide and seek – I'm always spotted.

Hey, look, I've discovered a new kind of human!

A shrinking forest

The Amazon rainforest isn't as large as it once was – 17 percent has been lost in the last 50 years. Humans have cut down large areas to use as farmland. This DEFORESTATION has harmful effects, including contributing to climate change. One GOOD thing is that the loss of rainforest is now SLOWING DOWN. We can CHEER that!

BEWARE!
Visitors must watch out for bloodsucking flies, biting caimans, MEGA painful bullet ants, aggressive piranhas in the rivers, giant anaconda snakes, deadly venomous stingrays and poison dart frogs. Oh, and vampire bats, too!

✦ VITAL FACTS ✦

How big is it? It's about twice the size of India (and that's a BIG country!)

Is it all in one country? No! 60 percent is in Brazil, but it spreads across EIGHT other countries as well

How many trees are there? No one knows, but one estimate is 390 billion

Does it have any towns and cities? Mostly small settlements, and a few cities such as Manaus and Pucallpa

Lost in the jungle!
Juliane Koepcke was 17 years old when the aircraft she was in broke apart in a VIOLENT STORM. She fell 3 km to the ground, strapped to her seat, suffering only cuts and bruises. Unable to find any other survivors, Juliane walked through the jungle for 11 days following a small river, with only sweets to eat. She survived FLESH-EATING MAGGOTS and cold nights until she eventually met some fishermen who took her to a town.

AURORA BOREALIS

The aurora borealis is not a place you can visit, it's a PHENOMENON, and a truly spectacular one. Sometimes called the NORTHERN LIGHTS, it's a natural display of glowing light in the night sky seen in the far north, especially towards the Arctic Circle. So, what ON EARTH IS GOING ON?

✦ VITAL FACTS ✦

What exactly is the aurora? A shimmering curtain of colourful lights in the night sky

Where can it be seen? In northern countries such as Norway, Sweden, Finland, Canada and Iceland

Is it only in the north? The southern hemisphere has the Southern Lights, called the Aurora Australis

What colours can be seen? Green and purple are the most common

Aurora fact-blast

✦ When there is a solar storm (MASSIVE EXPLOSIONS on the Sun), the aurora can be seen further south, in places like the UK and USA

✦ There was a huge magnetic solar storm in 1859. The sky was so bright that people could read books outside at night

✦ To see the Northern Lights you need a cloudless sky away from light pollution. You do NOT need sunglasses, a big hat or a cheese toastie...

What causes the aurora?

OK, here's what happens:

1. The Sun gives off hot, magnetized particles called SOLAR WIND that SLAM into Earth's outer atmosphere at over 1.5 MILLION KPH!

2. This collision causes particles in our atmosphere to heat up and GLOW around the poles

3. Different gases in the atmosphere give off different COLOURS when heated, e.g. oxygen produces green light

Pah, I need sleep, not a space disco!

SALAR DE UYUNI

You might think that a very FLAT place is not really interesting. But what if it was PURE WHITE? What if its wet surface acted like a GIANT MIRROR, creating extraordinary reflections? What if it was the BIGGEST SALT FLAT in the world?

◆ VITAL FACTS ◆

What is a salt flat? It's the flat, dried-out bed of a large lake, covered in a hard salt crust

Where is it? It's high in the Andes Mountains in Bolivia

How big is it? Huge! It's bigger than Cyprus and can be seen from space

Is there a lot of salt here? Oh yes, about 10 BILLION TONNES of it!

Is it completely empty? There are no trees but there are two rocky 'islands' with large cacti

SHOW-OFF fun at the Salar de Uyuni

- Many people come here to create funny photos. For example, a person in the distance can look tiny, like they are standing in the palm of your hand
- In a wet area, you can see the sky and mountains perfectly reflected in the surface
- You can stay in a local hotel made from blocks of SALT

How on EARTH can there be a huge flat place in the middle of some mountains?

Good question. About 40,000 years ago there was a giant lake here, but the water evaporated over time, leaving behind the salt it contained. The salt forms weird polygon patterns in places.

I present my little brother and sister!

Salty facts

- ◆ Big flocks of flamingos come to the salt flats to breed each year
- ◆ The salt contains lithium, used to make phone and laptop batteries
- ◆ Salar de Uyuni featured in *Star Wars: The Last Jedi*

ICEBERG A23A

Some things are big, some things are huge and some are IMMENSE. And then there's Iceberg A23a. It's twice as large as London and would take over two days to walk across. This flat island of ice, known as a tabular iceberg, is a gigantic section of an ice shelf that broke away from Antarctica decades ago. It's the biggest one on the planet.

Where did this white beast come from?

Like many other icebergs, A23a started out as a glacier slowly moving towards the sea. As the ice melted, pieces broke off – and this is one GIANT of a piece! It calved (broke away) in 1986 and was stuck on the seafloor for over 30 YEARS! It began moving again once the ice became thinner due to melting and erosion by the ocean.

A23a FACT FEAST

- Most of the berg is underwater – only 15 percent is visible
- It's slowly breaking up as it melts and is battered by waves
- Its edges are full of massive ice caves and arches
- It's made of fresh water and dust
- The glacier that formed the berg picked up rock particles containing minerals. Now, as the berg melts, tiny ocean creatures feed on the minerals

Watch out, ships!

Famously, the *Titanic* crashed into an iceberg in 1912 and was sunk. It would be REALLY hard not to notice this monster as you're sailing along! Some people actually tow small bergs called growlers to land and then melt the ice to sell for drinks. A23a would make a LOT of drinks...

Coming right up!

✦ VITAL FACTS ✦

How big? 74 km long and 60 km wide

How many football pitches is that? Over half a million

How heavy? Nearly one trillion tonnes (twice the weight of all humans on Earth!)

How thick is the ice? 400 m

Is it moving? Yes, very slowly!

Erm, we may need to turn around...

SAHARA DESERT

The mighty Sahara Desert has a LOT to show off. The biggest hot desert in the world has ENORMOUS sand dunes, VAST rocky plains sculpted by the wind, LONG mountain ranges crossed by remote valleys, BEAUTIFUL green oases where trees are fed by underground rivers, and much more, too!

Handy sandy facts

- Only one-fifth of the desert surface is sand – the rest is rock
- When strong winds blow sand into rocks, they wear away and become… MORE SAND!
- There are 'singing dunes' in the desert, so-called because wind-blown sand sometimes hums as it falls down steep edges
- Sand dunes are constantly moving, blown by winds, which causes many people to get lost in the desert
- A large amount of reddish Saharan dust is blown high into the air. Some of it travels thousands of kilometres, propelled by strong winds, and causes orange skies to be seen around the world

Just nipping to the shops – see you in three weeks!

Who needs clothes?

The animals that live in the desert – like lizards, scorpions and silver ants – are adapted to survive in hot, dry conditions. One of the most interesting is the naked mole rat, which has no fur and stays underground to keep cool. It also runs backwards incredibly fast to escape predators like foxes. And it EATS ITS OWN POO to save water. Sensible.

Want to try some?

How much sand is there in the Sahara?

It's not just a big number, but the WHOPPER OF WHOPPERS! Of course, no one knows the exact answer, but scientists estimate 1.5 septillion grains, which is 1,500,000,000,000,000,000,000,000.

58 grains, 59 grains, 60, 61, 62...

✦ VITAL FACTS ✦

How big is the desert? It covers about 9.4 million square km. That's larger than Australia and 16 times bigger than France!

Where is it? It stretches across 11 countries in North Africa

How long would it take to drive across? About 2 days, travelling non-stop, to cover 4,800 km

How big are the sand dunes? Up to 180 m high

How hot does it get? Very hot: often over 40°C (and the sand can reach a sizzling 80°C)

Oh well, only 249 km to go...

Mauro's marathon goes wrong

In 1994, an Italian policeman called Mauro Prosperi entered one of the world's toughest running races, the Marathon des Sables, which is 250 km across the Sahara. Mauro became lost in a sandstorm and went off course. He was lost for 10 days, surviving by eating small animals. When he was eventually found by local travellers, he was arrested as a spy!

GIANT'S CAUSEWAY

This strange landscape looks like it's made by humans, but it's ENTIRELY NATURAL! It's a spectacular feature of volcanic rocks on the Atlantic coast of Northern Ireland in the UK, and most of them are HEXAGON-SHAPED. WHAAT! How did THAT happen?

◆ VITAL FACTS ◆

What are the rocks? They are interlocking columns of a stone called basalt

How many columns are there? About 40,000

Are they all hexagonal? Most are, with six sides, but some have four, five, seven, or eight sides

How tall are the columns? The biggest ones, set in cliffs, are 25 m tall

So, you want to know how this landscape was formed, eh?

Well, there are two explanations of how the Giant's Causeway was created. YOU decide which is true!

◆ Version 1 ◆

About 60 million years ago, there was a lot of underground volcanic activity in this area. Liquid lava flowed upwards through cracks in the ground, then began to cool. As the hot fluid basalt cooled, it CRACKED, like drying mud, forming stone columns.

Goo-goo go home.

◆ Version 2 ◆

An Irish giant by the name of Finn McCool was challenged to a fight by an ENORMOUS Scottish hulk called Benandonner. McCool accepted the invitation and built a stone causeway across the sea so he could take on his challenger. But upon discovering the TERRIFYING SIZE of the giant, McCool fled. To escape, his wife Oona disguised him as a baby. Benandonner came across to fight, but when he saw the size of the baby, he was convinced that McCool would be too big to take on. He ran back home, ripping up the causeway so he could not be followed.

✦ VITAL FACTS ✦

Where is the mountain? It's high in the Andes Mountains in Peru

How high is it? 5,200 m

Are the stripes natural? Yes, they are layers of different minerals

Does it really have seven colours? Most people say it has seven, just like a rainbow, but the mountain's official website mentions four colours

Visitors WATCH OUT

- ◆ It's a very long drive and a tough walk to reach the mountain
- ◆ The air at 5,000 m has reduced oxygen so some people suffer altitude sickness
- ◆ It can be COLD at the top
- ◆ On the plus side, you might see lovely ALPACAS AND LLAMAS

RAINBOW MOUNTAIN

Mountains are usually grey, or white if they are covered in snow, but this one is STRIPY and MULTI-COLOURED! The local name for the peak is Vinicunca, the Mountain of Seven Colours. It has only been visible since 2013 when a glacier melted, revealing this remarkable sight.

No selfies!

Meanie.

Why the stripes?

Scientists think that these rocks were created by layers of sand, mud and other substances being compacted UNDERWATER over long periods of time. When two giant tectonic plates CRUNCHED together, Earth's crust was forced upwards, creating the Andes and Rainbow Mountain. So, these stripes are seabed layers that have been lifted up over 5 km! Over time, the different chemical substances in the rocks reacted with the weather to form multiple colours.

YOU CHOOSE!

And now it's YOUR turn to decide where to go, what to do, and who to go with as you TRAVEL the WORLD in your imagination...

Be my guest!
WHO would you take with you to...

a) Watch a **volcano** erupt?
b) Ski in the **Dolomites**?
c) Float in the **Dead Sea**?
d) Play ice golf on **Lake Baikal**?

Earth show-off ratings
What SCORE OUT OF 10 would you give these places?

a) A **mountain** covered in cherry blossom
b) A hot bubbling geothermal **mud pool**
c) A frozen **sea**
d) A **forest** full of giant redwood trees
e) A shell **beach**
f) A set of thundering **river rapids**
g) A booming **geyser**

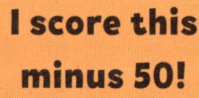

I score this minus 50!

Choose a challenge
Which of these would you LOVE to do? (And which would you HATE to do?)

a) Climb **Mount Everest**
b) Surf the giant waves at **Nazaré**
c) Scuba dive at the **Great Barrier Reef**
d) Kayak down the **Amazon River**

Take me to your leading destination!

If an ALIEN landed near you, where would you take them LOCALLY to show off the planet? Where would you NOT take them?

Your favourite?

What's the best NATURAL PLACE that you have ever been to?

✦ WHAT ABOUT YOU? ✦

The world is your OYSTER!
If you could go ANYWHERE on the planet for the day, where would you choose?

You're in charge!
If you had the power to help protect any of the places in this book, what would you do?

✦ TOUGH CHOICE ✦
If you could visit one of these from each pair, which would it be? Ask a friend, too!

Mountain OR **cave?**

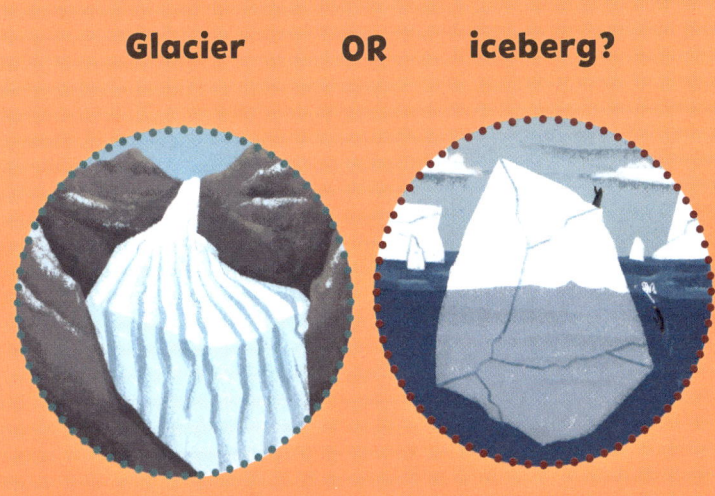

Glacier OR iceberg?

Waterfall OR coral reef?

Rainforest OR desert?

QUIZ ANSWERS

HIGH AND MIGHTY, PAGE 9

1. 40 days
2. iron 
3. bombs 
4. cold and smelly 
5. underwater 
6. in a cornfield 
7. Romans 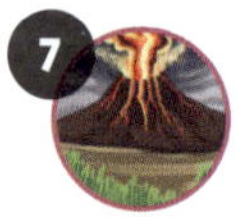
8. ski 
9. staircase 

DEEP AND DANGEROUS, PAGE 35

1. by motorbike
2. an underground river 
3. burned up on impact 
4. the Eiffel Tower 
5. a plastic bag 
6. earthquakes 
7. sulphur 

WET AND WILD, PAGE 23

1. Portugal
2. ice golf 
3. skeletons 
4. pink dolphins 
5. south to north 
6. the Devil's Throat 
7. salt 
8. cotton castle 
9. tiny microbes 

VAST AND VARIED, PAGE 47

1. bullet ant
2. gas 
3. take funny photos 
4. water and dust 
5. orange skies 
6. cooled lava 
7. a glacier

GLOSSARY

Avalanche a fast and dangerous fall of a large amount of snow down a mountainside

Causeway a raised path across a low, wet place

Chasm a very large, deep, steep-sided hole in the ground

Crampons metal spikes attached to boots for climbing over ice

Deforestation when trees are removed across a large area

Dik-dik a small antelope from Africa

Dugong a large sea mammal

Erosion when something is worn away by weather over time

Evaporate when liquid water dries up, turning to gas

Evolution the gradual development of animals over time, helping them survive

Geothermal heat energy from water generated by hot rocks underground

Gorge a steep-sided deep valley found in hilly countryside

Iguana a large lizard, usually green in colour

Indigenous being the first to live in, or come from, a particular place

Marooned when a person is left abandoned, usually on a small island

Meteorite a lump of rock or metal that has fallen to Earth from space

Microbe a very small living thing

Minerals solid substances found in Earth's surface, such as iron or quartz

Observatory a building containing a large telescope and other equipment for studying the universe

Phenomenon a remarkable event or happening that's seen by people

Polygon a shape with many sides

Polyp a small, tube-shaped animal found in the sea

Reef an area of rock or coral found in shallow water

Salt flat a large, very flat area of hard salt where a lake has dried up

Sea cucumber a simple type of sea creature with a long, often colourful body

Tectonic plate one of the huge slabs of rock that form the surface of Earth

Tributary a river that flows into a larger river

Venomous an animal that contains venom, a powerful poison

Volcanic bomb a lump of very hot rock thrown out by a volcano

Wingsuit a special suit with extended sleeves to catch air, used by skydivers and BASE jumpers

INDEX

A
A23A 52-53
Amazon 28, 48-49
Aurora Borealis 50

B
base jumping 20, 42

C
canyons 36-37
cars 25, 37
caves 38
chasms 30, 38
cliffs 14-15
Cliffs of Moher 14
climbers 10-11, 15, 16
Clipperton Island 41
coral reefs 26-27
craters 39
crevasses 13

D
Dead Sea 31
deserts 20, 54-55
Dolomite Mountains 21
Drakensberg 15

E
Egypt 29
El Capitan 15
environmental problems 11, 27, 45, 47
erosion 42

F
floods 13

G
Galápagos Islands 41
geysers 44-45
Geysir 44
Giant's Causeway 56
glaciers 13, 52
gorges 36-37
Grand Canyon 36-37

H
hot springs 32, 44-45

I
ice 13, 25
icebergs 52-53

Iceland 41, 44
Iguazu Falls 30
islands 40-41

J
jungles 28, 48-49

K
Kjerag 15
Komodo Island 40

L
Lake Baikal 25
Lake Hillier 33
lakes 25, 31, 33, 51
living structures 26-27
Lofoten Islands 40

M
Mariana Trench 43
Mauna Kea 17
meteorites 39
motorbikes 37
Mount Everest 10-11, 43
Mount Kilimanjaro 16
mountains 10-11, 12, 16-17, 21, 57

N
Nazaré 24
Northern Lights 50

O
Otzi the Iceman 21
oxygen 10, 16, 57

P
Padirac Cave 38
Pamukkale 32
Parícutin 18
Perito Moreno Glacier 13
pillars, stone 42, 56
pink lakes 33
pink lakes and beaches 40
Pohutu 45
polyps 26-27
Pompeii 19
poo 11, 41, 54

R
Rainbow Mountain 57
rainforests 28, 48-49
reefs 26-27
River Amazon 28
River Nile 29
rivers 28-29, 30, 36-37
rock formations 32, 42, 56-57

S
Sahara Desert 54-55
Salar de Uyuni 51
salt flats 51
salt lakes 31, 33
sand dunes 20, 54-55
sea 24, 26-27, 43
skiing 20
Skywalk 36
solar storms 50
Sossusvlei 20
staircases 21
stunts 37
surfing 24
survival stories 49, 55
swimming 31, 3

T
tectonic plates 10, 57
thermal springs 32, 44-45
tightrope walking 37
trenches 32, 43

U
Uluru 12

V
Vesuvius 19
volcanic springs 32
volcanoes (active) 18-19
volcanoes (inactive) 16-17

W
waterfalls 15, 30
waves 24
whirlpools 40
White Cliffs of Dover 14

Z
Zhangjiajie pillars 42